HEBREWS

THE DAILY DISCIPLINE OF A DEVOTED LIFE

Copyright © 2016 by Jeremy McQuoid

First published in Great Britain in 2016

The right of Jeremy McQuoid to be identified as the Author of this Work has been asserted by him in accordance with the Copyright, Designs and Patents Act 1988.

British Library Cataloguing in Publication Data
A record for this book is available from the British Library

ISBN: 978-1-910587-61-4
Designed by Diane Warnes
Printed in the UK

10Publishing, a division of 10ofthose.com
Unit C, Tomlinson Road, Leyland, PR25 2DY, England
Email: info@10ofthose.com
Website: www.10ofthose.com

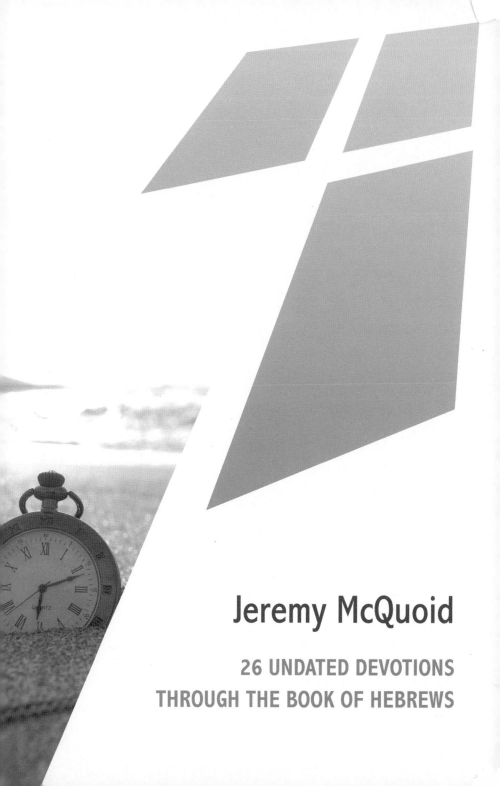

Jeremy McQuoid

**26 UNDATED DEVOTIONS
THROUGH THE BOOK OF HEBREWS**

INTRODUCTION

'Don't give up!' That is the message behind the letter to the Hebrews. It was written to a group of Jewish Christians who had left their Jewish heritage behind to follow Jesus, but they had begun to regret that decision. Judaism had centuries of tradition, a magnificent temple, and priests who wore splendid robes and offered sacrifices and incense. The Jewish temple was a spectacular sight.

By contrast these new Christians met together in humble home groups. They worshipped a Saviour they could not see, and were being severely persecuted by Jewish friends and relatives who believed they had betrayed their Jewish roots to follow a 'sect', a distortion of Judaism.

So the writer wants to encourage these Christians that what they have in Jesus is far greater than the Judaism they left behind. Jesus is greater than all the heroes of the Old Testament put together. He is greater than angels (ch. 1), greater than Moses (ch. 3), greater than Joshua (ch. 4), and greater than Aaron the priest (chs 5–10, the heart of the book). In fact all these Old Testament heroes and institutions are pointing to Jesus. Christ is the fulfilment of all the Old Testament was pointing to. To turn your back on Jesus is to reject the Son of God, the Saviour whose blood was worth more than all the animal sacrifices of the Old Testament put together.

'Don't give up on Jesus' is a timely message for Christians today. We face an onslaught from atheists telling us our Jesus is make-believe and our scriptures are full of myths. We live in a world where what you can see and touch is all that matters, and it is difficult to live your life for an unseen Saviour.

But in the challenges we face as believers today Hebrews keeps telling us, 'fix [your] eyes on Jesus, the author and perfecter of our faith' (Heb. 12:2). Walk by faith, not by sight. Jesus is God's final word. He is the ruler over all creation. But he is not only God the Son, he is fully human. His blood rescues us from sin forever, and he sympathises with our frailties and weeps in our pain.

Christ is totally sufficient, not just to save you, but for every doubt, every failing, and every tear you shed. Following him will bring rejection today, yes, but glory tomorrow. So don't give up. The best is yet to be!

I remember visiting the British Houses of Parliament a few years ago. They allowed me to sit in an upstairs gallery and view a debate in progress. I had been used to seeing on the television Prime Minister's Questions, when the atmosphere was electric, and every seat was taken. But on this quiet Wednesday afternoon there were about six MPs, who were almost lost in the giant halls, and were debating something about electricity prices. I enjoyed the visit, but this small group of MPs were a sideshow. The Prime Minister was the main event.

Hebrews opens with a bang as the writer tells his Jewish readers that their Old Testament heroes, the prophets, were actually a sideshow to the main event. They were important, but their value was in pointing beyond their own times to the coming of God's Messiah. And the decisive moment of God's salvation plan had now come.

Jesus of Nazareth was not just another prophet; he was and is God's Son, the 'exact representation of [God's] being' (v. 3). Like the image of the emperor stamped on Roman coins, God's character was so stamped on Jesus that to see him was really to see the Father – the God of Israel who appeared to Moses from a burning bush.

This Jesus is not just another Hebrew prophet. He is the one to whom all the prophets were pointing. He is the creator of the universe, and humanity's saviour. He came to shed his blood and provide purification for sin. Today he sits in heaven (v. 3) – the act of sitting showing that he has completed the work of redemption.

'Take the world, but give me Jesus' is how the hymn-writer Fanny Crosby put it. All God's plans for the whole of creation revolve around Jesus. He is worth every sacrifice it takes to follow him. Everything else in life is sinking sand compared to what Paul called 'the surpassing greatness of knowing Christ Jesus my Lord, for whose sake I have lost all things. I consider them rubbish, that I may gain Christ' (Phil. 3:8).

REFLECTION

Is there anything that matters more to you than Jesus? What other 'treasures' do you need to let go of to 'gain Christ'?

'I believe in angels' sang the Swedish pop group Abba. For many today, angels are only the figment of an overactive imagination. But for the Old Testament Jews, angels were awesome beings who provoked fear in their hearts. Jewish tradition said it was angels who delivered the Ten Commandments to Moses at Sinai.

So it was a huge thing for the writer to say that Jesus is greater than the angels. But that is the theme of this amazing passage: Jesus is greater than angels:

- **In his identity.** Angels are 'servants' of God (v. 7), but Jesus is God's Son (v. 5). Before Jesus became human at Bethlehem, he enjoyed an eternal relationship with the Father. The writer calls Jesus the 'firstborn' (v. 6), which does not mean he was created, but that Christ rules over creation. Jesus is the eternal Son who holds the cosmos in his hands.

- **In his purity.** Jesus 'loved righteousness and hated wickedness' (v. 9). The angels are holy, but Jesus is the essence of purity. Purity is considered quaint and old-fashioned today, but purity delights God, and Jesus' purity is the theme of angel worship. God calls us to reflect Christ in the purity of our thoughts and motives.

- **In his eternity.** Jesus' throne is 'for ever and ever' (v. 8) and his years 'will never end' (v. 12). We limited humans have only ever known time, and see our brief lifespan as a series of moments. But Jesus is eternal, and stands outside of time. He has always existed, and will always be!

- **In his authority.** This passage says Jesus has a throne and a kingdom for ever (v. 8), and one day God will put all his enemies under his feet (v. 13). We cannot fully see Jesus' authority in our world now, but in a coming day, all of creation – angels and demons and human beings – will bow and accept that Jesus is Lord.

Whatever we think of angels, we should fall down in wonder at the Lord Jesus Christ, the eternal Son, for whom the universe exists, and who holds our breath in his hand.

REFLECTION

Have you lost your awe for Christ? Are you purifying your thoughts and motives (see Phil. 4:8)?

You may remember the various colour codes that the American government used in the aftermath of 9/11. Green meant a 'low' risk of terrorist attacks; blue meant 'guarded' or remain vigilant; yellow meant an 'elevated' risk; orange meant a 'high' risk; and red meant a 'severe' risk – in other words, start filling your underground bunker with tins of baked beans because World War Three is about to start!

Hebrews is interspersed with red-level warning passages, because rejecting Jesus is such a huge issue. The most famous warning is in the middle of this passage: 'how shall we escape if we ignore such a great salvation?' (v. 3). The writer warns the Christians about the danger of drifting (v. 1), like a raft floating away from its moorings while no one is paying attention.

We may not think that we will ever give up on Jesus. But there is always the danger we might simply neglect him. I have seen many young Christians full of passion for Christ. But then family comes along, work gets busy, and building a home, making money and pursuing hobbies – all legitimate interests – start to crowd in. And little by little their faith gets eroded, like waves beating away at a rocky coastline, until one morning they wake up and they have no real desire for Jesus at all.

The problem with drifting is that it never seems serious at the time. We live our lives on code green, probably thinking, 'I should be reading my Bible or praying a bit more', but never actually getting round to it. The warnings in Hebrews are stark for that very reason. Every backward step we take from focusing on Jesus – worshipping him, loving him supremely, obeying his commands, and thirsting for his glory – should be coded red, because we are stepping away from our 'salvation' (v. 3). This is serious business.

The warnings in Hebrews will end with the story of Esau selling his birthright for a pot of stew, and walking away weeping (ch. 12). It will feel 100 times worse if we drift away from Jesus. We would be casually drifting away from God's Son, the creator of the cosmos, who died for us; drifting away from eternal salvation; and drifting away from a miraculous gospel story that was 'testified to … by signs, wonders … and gifts of the Holy Spirit' (v. 4).

If you are living on code green right now, and sense your apathy growing, shift the warning levels up a couple of notches, get back on your knees in repentance, and ask your gracious God to restore the joy of your salvation (Ps. 51).

REFLECTION

Are you drifting in your faith? Do you have an accountability partner?

Bono, the lead singer of the Irish rock group U2, said that his most moving moment did not come on stage at a concert, but quietly in the pews of a Dublin church, thinking about the Son of God becoming a baby. He said, 'The idea that God ... would seek to explain himself is amazing enough. That he would seek to explain himself by becoming a child born in poverty and straw ... I just thought: "Wow!"'[1]

Jesus is great not just because he is the Son of God, but especially because he became fully human. Jesus the man is:

- **Our pioneer.** Jesus is the fulfilment of Psalm 8, which teaches that man's ultimate destiny is to rule the world. Christ has blazed a trail for us to follow. His death and resurrection mean he has destroyed the powers of sin that frustrate this current creation (Rom. 8), and he will rule over a future new heavens and new earth as a 'second Adam'. And if you follow him, the amazing truth is that you will rule at his side in a new world. Whatever struggles you are facing right now, keep your heart fixed on the glory to come.

- **Our brother.** Jesus was not 50% human. He was 100% human (and 100% divine). He experienced all the emotions we face, and was 'made like his brothers in every way' (v. 17). He opened himself to pain and temptation, to tears and frustration. Jesus is no 'deist' god who stands aloof from his creatures, but a God who knows us thoroughly – trial for trial, bruise for bruise, tear for tear. Draw near to the God who has drawn near to you.

- **Our deliverer.** We need more than a God who can sympathise with us. We need one who can rescue us from death, this power that the Devil holds over us (v. 14). But to rescue us from death, the eternal Son of God had to die himself. His death has a unique power to 'free' (v. 15) those who are paralysed by a fear of death. We don't need to fear death anymore, because he has conquered its power over us. Hallelujah!

REFLECTION

Consider these words: 'He [Jesus] became like us, so that we could become like him' (Athanasius, a fourth-century bishop of Alexandria).

[1] *Bono: in conversation* (New York: Riverhead Books, 2005), 124-5.

Boxers aren't usually known for their humility, and the most famous of them all – Cassius Marcellus Clay, who became known as Muhammad Ali following his conversion to Islam – was not known for his bashfulness. He called himself 'the Greatest'. While assessing greatness is always subjective, Ali's gloves rightfully hang in the boxing Hall of Fame. Not only was he a great sportsman, but he became an icon in the 60s for refusing to go to Vietnam and eloquently proclaiming his pacifist sympathies around American universities.

This passage is all about greatness. The writer takes the standout hero of the Jewish faith – Moses – and compares him to Christ. He does not denigrate Moses. Moses was a 'servant' of God (v. 5), but Jesus is the Son. Moses led the people of Israel to an earthly promised land, but Jesus is leading us to our 'heavenly calling' (v. 1).

Moses rescued Israel from Egypt, but Jesus has rescued us from more ultimate enemies – sin, death and hell. Moses spilt the blood of the symbolic Passover Lamb, but Jesus has shed his own blood to redeem us. Moses led the people through the sea, but we have been baptised into Christ, and our identity is in Christ.

Moses was the mediator, bringing the law of God to Israel. But Jesus is a greater mediator. He is our great 'high priest' (v. 1), who represents us before the throne of God every moment of every day. Jesus is 'undiminished deity and perfect humanity united without confusion in one person forever', as the Chalcedonian Creed puts it. He is our link to the Father, as we offer every prayer in his name.

Moses was great, but Jesus is the greatest. Don't look to anyone or anything else as your inspiration for living. Don't look to your spouse or your children, to your career progress or your bank account. Don't look to a sports team or a dream home. Don't even look to the pastor or elders of your church, or some Christian teacher you listen to online who inspires you.

People will always disappoint – even Moses struck a rock in anger and therefore was kept out of the Promised Land (Num. 20:1–13). But 'Jesus Christ is the same yesterday and today and for ever' (Heb. 13:8). He alone is a solid rock in the midst of sinking sand.

REFLECTION

Are you looking to anything outside of Jesus to give you meaning and purpose?

11

World War One was famously called 'the war to end all wars', yet ironically, only twenty years later, the world descended into World War Two. It is as though we learned nothing from the bodies of young soldiers scattered over the trenches of the Somme.

Here the writer wants to make sure that these Hebrew Christians, who were showing signs of deserting Christ, did not forget the lesson of their forefathers in the desert. Then bodies were strewn across the Wilderness because of those who turned their backs on the God who rescued them from Egyptian slavery.

'Today, if you hear his voice, do not harden your hearts' (v. 7), implores the writer, as he reminds his readers of Israel's debacles at Massah and Meribah (Ex. 17:7). The frightening truth was that Israel's rebellion then made God swear that his people – the very ones he had rescued from Egypt, and signed a covenant with at Sinai – would not 'enter my rest' (v. 11). Rest in the Old Testament context meant release from struggle and settlement in the Promised Land. Rest in our context means bringing our earthly labours to an end and entering God's new world.

It is possible to be part of a believing community, yet have an 'unbelieving heart' (v. 12). It is possible to attend church, read your Bible daily, and even have a systematic prayer life, without being truly transformed by responding to the promptings of the Holy Spirit through the living Word of God.

And if you continue to fill your life with Christian ritual and discipline, without allowing God's Word to penetrate and change you, and move you to heartfelt service and devotion, your heart becomes hard. There is no worse place to be than to be impervious to God's voice.

This passage is a warning we all need to hear now, before we slide into hardness of heart. It applies even to those of us who open our Bibles every day, and read devotional guides! Don't assess your relationship with God by how much ritual or discipline there is in your life, but by how much transformation there is in your soul.

Are you really listening to God? Are you really obeying him? Or do you need to ask the Spirit to circumcise your heart again (to use a phrase from Deut. 10:16), until you are sensitive to every command and urging of scripture?

REFLECTION

Ponder the words of this hymn: 'Search me, O God, and know my heart today; try me, O Saviour, know my thoughts, I pray' (James E. Orr).

It's difficult to find rest, isn't it? We live such busy lives with work demands and taxiing our children to sports teams and music lessons, and then we want to be faithful at church. How can we find rest in such a hectic world?

Well, this passage talks about God taking a rest from all his creation work on the seventh day. And the seventh day then becomes a glorious metaphor of how we can enter God's rest. The call to come to Christ is pictured as entering God's rest.

First, the Old Testament hero switches from being Moses to Joshua, who was Israel's military general on their conquest of Canaan. And during that conquest God kept promising his people 'rest', which, in that context, meant rest from war and enemies to take up their inheritance in the Promised Land.

Then the metaphor grows bigger, extending from the seventh day of Genesis 2, through Joshua's military rest, right into the ministry of Christ, where he invites people to 'enter that rest' (v. 11). Our good works cannot make us right with God, and Christ's invitation is to stop trying to earn favour with God and instead rest on the finished work of Christ at the cross, which provides forgiveness and peace with the Father – 'for anyone who enters God's rest also rests from his own work, just as God did from his' (v. 10).

Ironically the writer tells his readers to 'strive' (v. 11, ESV) or 'make every effort to enter that rest' (v. 11, NIV). The Christian life is a combination of resting in the finished work of Christ, and striving to serve and please God before we take up our ultimate 'rest' in a new heavens and new earth. The writer was warning these Hebrews that they had not really entered God's rest if they were not striving to please Jesus.

Salvation is a 'now, but not yet' reality. We experience God's rest in part in this life, believing in Christ for forgiveness of our sins. But we await our final, ultimate rest, where we will not need to struggle to please God – it will come naturally as glorified saints – and we will take up the inheritance God has promised for us, one that 'can never perish, spoil or fade' (1 Pet. 1:4).

So don't be worried if the spiritual 'rest' you enjoy today doesn't feel very restful! Your sins are forgiven; you have peace with God – if you are trusting in Christ. But the battle with the sinful nature will continue in this life until you enter the glory prepared for you since before the world began. In that battle, you need to take up God's Word daily, which is 'living and active. Sharper than any double-edged sword ...' (v. 12). The Word is like a scalpel, painfully opening up dark desires and sins you did not know you had. But his Word will weed out the corrupt to make way for the fruit of the Spirit!

REFLECTION

Are you trusting in Christ's finished work, or are you still trying to earn favour with God?

Recently I was visiting a friend in hospital whose family were not churchgoers. When I arrived at the bedside, my friend said, 'There's my priest!' It was the only way he could think of to explain to his family what I did for a living. I'm not a priest (at least not in the sense that he meant), but who a priest is and what a priest does is at the heart of Hebrews, and this passage teaches us three things about Jesus the Priest:

1. He sympathises with us. Jesus 'has been tempted in every way, just as we are' (4:15). He is not some shadowy figure we venerate on stained-glass windows; he literally experienced humanness as fully as we do. Luke tells us he had to grow 'in wisdom and stature' (Lk. 2:52) in the normal human way. He was tired and hungry, hurt by Judas' betrayal, and wept deep tears at Lazarus' tomb. Christ faced loneliness having 'nowhere to lay his head' (Lk. 9:58), and never married. He was tempted repeatedly by Satan, and went through psychological turmoil followed by physical agony on the cross. So there is nothing you will or have ever passed through that he doesn't understand and feel deeply about. He became flesh not just to save you, but to understand you, and to be your inspiration in every triumph and trial of life.

2. He was chosen for us. The tribe of Levi was appointed by God to be high priests over Israel in perpetuity. That appointment was challenged by Israel, as Aaron showed his weakness in building the golden calf. But God has chosen Christ to be our High Priest forever. Unlike every human leader, Christ is the perfect representative to bring us to God, as he has never sinned or buckled to human pressure. Ultimately, all human leadership will let us down, but Christ never will.

3. He has power to save us. Jesus our Priest is the 'source of eternal salvation' (5:9). That salvation was won through power manifested in weakness: 'During the days of Jesus' life on earth, he offered up prayers and petitions with loud cries and tears' (5:7) He's not a priest who sits in a confessional booth or waves incense around. His eternal priesthood was sealed in the sweat of Gethsemane and the blood of Calvary. As Michael Card's song 'El Shaddai' puts it, God's 'most awesome work was done through the frailty of [his] son'.[2] It is a consistent truth in scripture that God's power is most manifest in our weakness.

REFLECTION

Think through Peter's instruction: 'Cast all your anxiety on him because he cares for you' (1 Pet. 5:7).

[2] Card, Michael,'El Shaddai', *Legacy* (Milk and Honey records, 1983)

DAY 9   **READ** Hebrews 5:11 – 6:12

Apparently sharks grow according to the size of tank you place them in. If you place them in a small tank, their growth will be stunted. Place them in the open sea, and they will reach their full potential. The concern in this passage is that the spiritual growth of these Jewish Christians has been stunted, and a lack of growth in the New Testament always leads to speculation over how real repentance was to begin with. This uncomfortable passage forces us to consider:

- **Are we making progress in the faith?** The writer can't continue his teaching on Melchizedek, begun in the previous verses, because his readers cannot take it. They should have progressed in the faith enough to be teachers now (5:12), but they love 'milk' rather than 'solid food' or meat, and have not trained themselves for deep teaching. It forces us to ask, 'Have we moved on from the basics of our faith? How hungry are we for deeper doctrine? What does it say about our faith if we've lost our hunger for Bible doctrine?'

- **The sign we are making progress is fruitfulness, not spiritual experience.** The writer talks about those who have been 'enlightened' (6:4), who have tasted something of the power of the Holy Spirit. They have rich Christian experience, but

that counts for nothing. It is like those who will say to Jesus on the Last Day, '"...Lord, did we not ... in your name drive out demons and perform many miracles?" Then [he] will tell them plainly, "I never knew you. Away from me"' (Mt. 7:22–23). The proof we have truly trusted in Christ is that we become like 'land ... that produces a crop' that is 'useful' (6:7). Don't substitute your own powerful spiritual experiences for real obedience to God's Word.

- **Make sure we are growing in good works.** The writer talks about 'things that accompany salvation' (6:9), and mentions the Hebrews' love and the fellow believers they have helped as evidence that their salvation was authentic (6:10). We are not saved *by* good works, but we are saved *for* good works. Showing practical love, servant-heartedness, and personal witness are signs that we have been truly saved, and that the Holy Spirit is at work in us. Ephesians 2:10 reminds us that we were saved to pursue the good works that God 'prepared in advance for us to do'.

REFLECTION

What evidence is there in your life that you have been truly saved?

15

Please excuse this long reading, but this section about Melchizedek is where people tend to get bogged down in Hebrews! This is a complicated passage, but its teaching is core to the message of the book. Let's remember the big picture of Hebrews: the writer is telling Jewish Christians, on the verge of giving up their faith and going back to Judaism, that Jesus is 'better' than all their Old Testament heroes and rituals. And this passage shows that Jesus is 'better' in three ways:

1. He is a better priest. The Old Testament priesthood was built on the family line of Aaron, who was sinful like the rest of us. He had to sacrifice for his own sins before he could sacrifice for the people. His priesthood was limited. But another shadowy figure appears in the Old Testament called Melchizedek. He was a priest who offered bread and wine to Abraham and blessed the patriarch, from whom the Levi and the Aaronic priesthood came (see Gen. 14:18–20). Melchizedek's name means 'king of righteousness' (7:2), and he prefigures the priesthood of Christ. Jesus is our king of righteousness, and was able to offer the perfect sacrifice for sin because, unlike Aaron, he was free from sin himself.

2. He is mediator of a better covenant. The old covenant was mediated by priests chosen on the basis of their family ancestry. But the covenant (the agreement between God and man) that Jesus has established is so much better because it is based on 'the power of an indestructible life' (7:16). When Melchizedek appears as a priest in Genesis 14, he has no genealogy (7:3); it is as if he lives forever. Psalm 110:4 says that the Messiah will be 'a priest for ever, in the order of Melchizedek'. Aaron could only serve God's people for a generation. Jesus is a better priest because he represents us before God forever!

3. This covenant is based on a better sacrifice. There was something incomplete about Old Testament sacrifices. You had to continually offer lambs and bulls and goats, which could only symbolically forgive people. But Christ did not have to offer repeated sacrifices: 'He sacrificed for their sins once for all when he offered himself' (7:27). This once-for-all sacrifice fulfils all that the Old Testament order was pointing to but could not accomplish.

Jesus is a better priest, mediator of a better covenant, based on a better sacrifice. Worship him today!

REFLECTION

Thank God that all your sins, past, present and future, have been dealt with by the once-for-all sufficient sacrifice of Christ.

In Spielberg's movie *Close Encounters of the Third Kind*, unsuspecting bystanders come into contact with aliens, who seem to download into their minds a picture of a mountain. We don't understand why this mountain is important until the end of the movie, when each of these people travel to the mountain to discover that it is the chosen meeting place for the aliens and humans to get to know each other!

When Moses was on Mount Sinai, he was given instructions to build a tabernacle where animal sacrifices would be offered that allowed sinful Israelites to approach a holy God: 'See to it that you make everything according to the pattern shown you on the mountain' (v. 5). We aren't quite sure what that tabernacle ultimately points to until we come to Christ in the New Testament, or the new covenant. The Old Testament tabernacle was 'a copy and shadow of ... heavenly things' (v. 5, ESV).

The ceremonies connected with the tabernacle were all external. They could make an Israelite ceremonially right with God, but they could not change an Israelite's heart. God was using the picture of the Old Testament tabernacle, with its Holy Place and Most Holy Place (which regular Israelites could not enter), to teach us about our separation from God caused by sin. And our sin is something that cannot be taken away ceremonially – it demands a change of heart.

In verses 8–12 the writer quotes from Jeremiah 31, a pivotal passage that predicts how Christ would fulfil what the tabernacle ministry was foreshadowing. The Israelites could not keep the old covenant, based on the Ten Commandments: 'they did not remain faithful to my covenant' (v. 9). But God knew they couldn't, and had always planned to establish a new covenant: 'I will put my laws in their minds and write them on their hearts' (v. 10).

The new covenant would deal with our hearts in a way the old covenant never could. Jesus' blood cleanses our consciences and the Holy Spirit changes the desires of our hearts, so that we know God personally and have a new longing to serve him that Old Testament Israelites never enjoyed.

The days of killing lambs and goats are over. Jesus has now come to deal with the real, inner heart problem that separates us from God, and by his blood we can enter the Holy of Holies every time we pray, and have fellowship as forgiven sinners with the God of the universe!

REFLECTION

Make sure the ceremonies of your church don't deflect you from examining your own heart.

A picture says 1,000 words. The courts and curtains of the Old Testament tabernacle powerfully pictured the barrier between sinful man and a holy God. The closer you came to the Holy of Holies, the more precious the metal used – bronze for the outer courts, gold for the Most Holy Place.

No one was allowed into the Holy of Holies, except the high priest, once a year, on the Day of Atonement 'and never without blood, which he offered for himself and for the sins [of] the people' (v. 7). The high priest would light incense in the Holy Place – before entering through the seven-inch thick curtain into the Holy of Holies – so that the smoke from the incense would prevent him from beholding the throne of God, set in-between the wings of the cherubim.

What a powerful way of expressing the holiness of God. God wanted to dwell in the midst of his people – the tabernacle was at the centre of the Israelite camp – but only once a year, and following strict regulations, could the high priest dare to set foot in the holiest place of all. How could such a holy God have fellowship with such sinful people?

'When Christ came' (v. 11) are some of the richest words in scripture. Our righteous God/man has entered the holiest place of all in heaven. The earthly tabernacle was just a 'shadow' (8:5) teaching us how holy God's dwelling place in heaven is. Christ is worthy to enter the holiest place because he himself is supremely righteous, meeting all God's requirements.

But like the old covenant priests, he does not enter this heavenly sanctuary without blood. The blood he brings is worth more than all the lambs and goats and bulls of the old covenant put together – he enters 'by means of ... his own blood' (v. 12). Yet he does not have to offer sacrifices for his own sin, but for ours. And as he offers his blood at the mercy seat, through a great 'once for all' sacrifice, he secures for us an 'eternal redemption' (v. 12), meaning we can approach a holy God with full confidence and boldness.

This is glorious theology, but it's also incredibly practical, for 'the blood of Christ ... cleanse[s] our consciences from acts that lead to death, so that we may serve the living God' (v. 14). Our works lead to death because they cannot make up for our sin. But the Son of God, our perfect High Priest, has paid the price for our sin, and now we can serve God with pure hearts and a clear conscience – day after day his blood is cleansing us and making us right with God.

REFLECTION

How can you remind yourself of the extent of God's holiness, and the greatness of Christ's atonement?

Υou are probably familiar with the slogan for Sky TV – 'believe in better'. It was Rupert Murdoch's aim to take television onto a much higher plain through his satellite television company. Whether Murdoch has achieved his aims is a matter of conjecture.

But there is no doubt that the sacrifice of Christ is 'better', in every way imaginable, than the Old Testament sacrificial system that preceded it, and foreshadowed it. First, Jesus entered 'the greater and more perfect tabernacle' (v. 11). While Aaron brought blood into a tent in a desert, Jesus brought his blood right into the presence of God in heaven. Jesus' sacrifice brings you and me right into God's intimate, holy presence.

Second, Jesus entered that better tabernacle with better blood: not the blood of 'goats and bulls' (v. 13), but the blood of the perfect, eternal Son of God himself (vv. 12, 14). The one who died for us is of greater worth than all the sacrificial animals put together.

Third, the blood cleanses us more deeply than the Old Testament sacrifices did. The blood of sacrificial animals could only make you 'outwardly clean' (v. 13) in a ceremonial sense. But Jesus' blood has the power to 'cleanse our consciences' (v. 14). It genuinely removes guilt from our souls, for all our sins – past, present and future.

Fourth, we now have a better covenant. The sacrifices of the first covenant could not truly forgive sins. But now that Christ's sacrifice has fully dealt with sin, we can now receive 'the promised eternal inheritance' (v. 15) that Old Testament saints could only dream of.

Fifth, Jesus' sacrifice is better in the sense that it is more complete. While Old Testament priests had to offer their sacrifices 'again and again' (v. 25), as a sign that they could never properly deal with sin, now Christ 'has appeared once for all' (v. 26). In one mighty, sweeping act of salvation, as Jesus sheds his blood and takes the punishment for every sin committed in the history of the human race, Jesus brings complete salvation. And he will come again a second time, as the great sin conqueror, 'to bring salvation to those who are waiting for him' (v. 28). Salvation is not just a past experience on our conversion day; it is a future hope.

When you believe in Jesus, you 'believe in better'.

REFLECTION

You are saved in a most wonderful way, whether you understand all the dimensions of that salvation or not. But you will know Christ better if you take time to discover all that he has accomplished for you.

You may be feeling a little over-whelmed by now with this very detailed argument of how Jesus the priest fulfils all that the Old Testament ceremonies were pointing to. This passage is the conclusion of an argument the writer began back in chapter 5, and we're nearly at the end. From 10:19 onwards, the writer stops his exposition and starts his practical application, challenging us to be confident in Christ. But hang in there for one more passage!

The writer constantly quotes from the Old Testament to prove the supremacy of Christ. The Gospel is as much in the Old as the New Testament ('the New is in the Old concealed, the Old is in the New revealed'[3]). In verses 5–7 the writer quotes from Psalm 40:6–8 to show that a human being sacrificing himself was the real thing God wanted all along and to which all the Old Testament sacrifices were merely signposts: 'Sacrifice and offering you did not desire, but a body you prepared for me' (v. 5).

Even the Old Testament itself seemed to be saying that true forgiveness needs more than the repetitive, never-ending sacrifices and offerings prescribed in the law, and a mysterious human being emerges from Psalm 40 saying, 'I have come to do your will, O God' (v. 7) through this 'body you prepared for me'. Looking back through the lens of the New Testament, we can see how beautifully Christ has fulfilled this

psalm – he was given a body precisely so that he could sacrifice himself to deal with our sin. He willingly accepted the call of God to lay down his life, no matter how painful it would be.

Now that the ultimate sacrifice of Christ has arrived, the writer makes the bold claim that temple sacrifices are therefore obsolete. There is now no point in Jewish priests daily and repeatedly offering 'the same sacrifices, which can never take away sins' (v. 11). History records that, in AD 70, the Roman legions laid waste to the Jerusalem temple, and temple sacrifices have never been offered since that point – as if God were underlining the truth of Christ's all-sufficient sacrifice.

So where does all this leave us today? The writer has an interesting turn of phrase. Christ's death 'has made perfect for ever those who are being made holy' (v. 14). Our redemption is complete through Christ ('made perfect'), but we are called to grow in holiness every day ('sanctified', ESV) – to reflect in daily life who we are positionally in Christ. We are justified forever, but sanctification, growing in holiness, is an ongoing process.

REFLECTION

How are you doing in the process of sanctification? What is getting in the way?

[3] St Augustine, *Writings Against Pelagius*, chapter 27.

DAY 15

A preaching professor of mine told me that every sermon he has ever preached has the same outline. He asks three questions of every text: 'what?', 'so what?' and 'now what?' In other words, 'what does the passage say?', 'what does it mean?' and 'what difference should it make in my life?'

The writer to the Hebrews has spent ten chapters giving us the 'what', and it is glorious theology. Jesus is greater than anything the Old Testament has to offer. He is greater than angels, greater than Moses and Joshua, and greater than Aaron and the whole Old Testament priesthood and sacrificial system. But from this transitional paragraph until the end of the book, he applies the supremacy of Christ powerfully to our daily lives as Christians. This is the 'so what?' and 'now what?' of Hebrews!

Two key concepts dominate this paragraph. The first is the word 'confidence'. Jesus' once-for-all sacrifice for sin now gives us confidence to enter God's presence 'by a new and living way opened for us' (v. 20). This truth makes a tremendous difference to your prayer life.

What the high priest used to do with trembling hands once a year, as he dared to enter the Holy of Holies, we now do with confidence every time we pray in the name of Jesus. Our prayers ascend, unhindered, directly to God's throne – the holiest place in the universe – purified, as they are, by the blood of Christ. We are now invited to 'draw near' (v. 22) to the sanctuary of God, which used to be such a fearful place for Old Testament priests to go. Now it is home to us. As Mavis Ford's hymn 'I stand before the presence'[4] puts it, 'the holy of holies has become my dwelling place.'

The second key phrase is to 'hold unswervingly' (v. 23). The problem with these Jewish Christians is that their theology had cracked under pressure. The pagan culture around them and persecution from fellow Jews meant they were on the verge of walking away from Christ. So now that the writer has reminded them of the supremacy of Christ, they need to 'hold unswervingly' to the faith they profess.

We find ourselves in a similar position. Our secular world will tell us our Christ is a myth, our Bible is error-strewn, and our God is dead. But in the midst of that, we need to remind ourselves that Christ is worth our total allegiance. The Son of God, the Messiah who spilled his blood for us, is the meaning of life, and we need to hold tight to him, with full confidence that he will come again to claim the world as his own.

REFLECTION

Are you holding tight to your Christian convictions?

[4] Ford, Mavis, *I stand before the presence* (Authentic Publishing, 1980)

One of the best-selling books of our time is a guide for pregnant mothers called *What to Expect When You're Expecting.*[5] Amid the joy of having children, the book encourages new mums to be realistic about the chaos and sleepless nights that lie ahead. It's not all warm cuddles, and picture-perfect smiles!

This passage teaches us that Christians need to be realistic about the hard edges of our faith. While there is joy and peace, if we are expecting an easy ride we'll become disillusioned. There are three realities we need to be aware of:

1. The Day of Judgement. While liberals want to edit out divine judgement from scripture, you simply can't avoid it. This passage speaks of 'a fearful expectation of judgment and of raging fire that will consume the enemies of God' (v. 27). Alarmingly this warning is written to professing Christians. The writer says, 'If we deliberately keep on sinning' (v. 26) – if we have a laissez-faire approach to sin, don't want any Christian accountability, and grow apathetic about following Christ – then our Christian confession means nothing, and we, professing Christians, need to fear the flames! Do we need a wake-up call?

2. The call to suffer. The writer encourages his readers to remember back to days when they were willing to suffer for the Gospel. They stood by those in prison, and were willing to have their property confiscated. But this is in the past tense. It appears they are no longer willing to suffer for the faith. Suffering, whether it's physical, spiritual or psychological, is an expectation in the Christian life, not the unfortunate by-product of living in a fallen world. It is a sign that we are living authentically. It's what to expect when you are believing! Are you persevering in the midst of struggles right now, or toning down your commitment to Christ?

3. The hope of glory. It's not just the negatives of judgement and suffering we need to expect, but the hope of glory. Perhaps heaven seems distant to you right now, just as it seemed to these Hebrew Christians. They were encouraged to persevere 'so that when you have done the will of God, you will receive what he has promised' (v. 36). We have a glorious inheritance waiting for us beyond the stars. Don't let that hope dim in your heart. It is as certain as the rising of the sun. Your present trials will give way to a glory beyond imagination!

REFLECTION

How can you keep reminding yourself of the hope of glory?

  [5] Murkoff, Heidi, *What to Expect When You're Expecting* (Simon & Schuster, 1984)

The German pastor Dietrich Bonhoeffer left a huge impact in the concentration camp where he spent his last days. In fact one of his fellow inmates said, 'I've never met a man who was more certain God was listening to him when he prayed.' Bonhoeffer's faith in Christ inspired him to know that God was still there in the most godless place on earth.

Hebrews 11 is the great chapter of faith. And it begins with a definition: 'faith is being sure of what we hope for and certain of what we do not see' (v. 1). Faith is every way in which our lives display confidence in the unseen plans and power of God. This brief passage makes four great claims about faith. Faith:

1. Believes in a creator. 'By faith we understand that the universe was formed at God's command' (v. 3). While it takes faith to believe in a creator, it's not the kind of blind faith that Richard Dawkins suggests. Scientists tell us about the amazing fine-tuning in our universe. Imagine a giant universe-making machine with six dials, representing six forces like gravity and electromagnetism. Each of those dials have to be placed at exactly the point they are for life to be possible. If they change by a millimetre, life could not exist. Such facts fit well with a Christian worldview that teaches Christ sustains the cosmos by his powerful word.

2. Inspires you to worship. Abel's offering (v. 4) is contrasted to Cain's because Abel offered his best (the fat) of his flock to God while Cain offered just some of his fruit. Faith leads to wholehearted worship. King David said, 'I will not sacrifice to the LORD my God burnt offerings that cost me nothing' (2 Sam. 24:24). True worship is costly.

3. Stands out from the culture. Enoch (v. 5) appears briefly in the dark passage Genesis 5 that mentions the lives of various people and finishes with the repeated refrain 'and then he died'. Enoch stands out in that chapter because we're simply told he 'walked with God; then he was no more, because God took him away' (Gen. 5:24). Faith walks with God when the culture is walking in the opposite direction. If you are living by faith, you will be walking against the flow, but God is delighted with those who aren't looking for popularity, but for God's approval.

4. Looks forward to God's salvation. Noah (v. 7) built a boat for years and warned the people of impending judgement when there was no sign of it. But the day finally came when the ark was closed, the rain fell, the people perished, and believing Noah became king of a brave new world. And one day God will bring his final judgement, evil will be destroyed, and we will be kings and queens of a new world.

REFLECTION

If someone analysed your life, would they say you are living by faith?

READ Hebrews 11:8–31

We often link faith to a set of beliefs that we hold, yet this powerful chapter does not contain a confessional statement – it is action-packed. Faith is energetic, visionary, and risky. It is allowing what you believe about God to drive your whole life.

By faith Abraham left Ur of the Chaldees to go to an unknown land (v. 8), when he had nothing else to go on apart from God's Word: he 'went, even though he did not know where he was going.' In 1960 my father left a lucrative job in a Belfast engineering firm to be a missionary in Ethiopia. He knew nothing about Ethiopia other than what he had read. But our whole family history, including the lady my father was to marry, was to be dictated by this call of God – a call that seemed absurd to my dad's boss. The church Dad planted in Addis Ababa has now mushroomed, by God's grace, to take in more than 12,000 believers, in over 80 congregations!

But faith isn't just about adventure; it's about sacrifice (v. 17), as God calls Abraham to sacrifice his beloved son, Isaac. It was Abraham's hope in God's power to raise the dead that led him to give up his precious son. Faith often involves losing out in this world so we can find joy and reward in the next. The repeated refrain in this chapter is that people of faith lived as 'aliens and strangers on earth' (v. 13). The more smug we are in the West, the less likely we are to be living by faith!

Faith affects how parents raise their children (v. 23). By faith Moses' parents discerned that Moses was no ordinary child, so they broke the law of Egypt, and risked their lives, to hide Moses in the bulrushes. As a father of three small boys, I want to look at them with their struggles and sins, and dream kingdom dreams for them. But that involves me as a parent investing in their spiritual, moral and educational development. Does your faith inspire you to dream big kingdom dreams for your kids and grandkids, or do you *just* want them to be healthy, wealthy and happy?

Faith is an action word that propels you to leave your comfort zone – like Moses leaving the palaces of Egypt – and discover God, often in the desert experiences of life. Faith makes you vulnerable to God, but it's also powerful – powerful enough to conquer kingdoms, administer justice and bring down the walls of Jericho! Don't leave home without it!

REFLECTION

Has your faith led to action?

Faith is not a popular word in our culture. Richard Dawkins says, 'Faith is the great cop-out' – it avoids the need to think and evaluate evidence. He quotes Carl Sagan, who allegedly said, 'By all means let's be open-minded, but not so open-minded that our brains fall out!' The writer to the Hebrews thinks the exact opposite. People of faith are the most courageous, realistic people on the planet.

This chapter is like a hymn in praise of faith, and this passage acts like the crescendo of the hymn. Faith transforms the human experience. Faith:

- **Gives power to the weak.** The writer names some of the great heroes of faith, but there should be an asterisk next to each one, because they had great failings alongside great triumphs. Gideon was a coward, Samson a womaniser, Jephthah made a rash vow and David committed adultery! These were men of clay, but when they exercised faith, God turned their weakness into strength. And he does the same with you and me, with all our baggage, sins and frailties. Faith gives power to the weak.

- **Gives meaning to our suffering.** Special praise is reserved not for those who conquered kingdoms and quenched the fury of the flames, but for those who endured terrible suffering by faith: those who were 'tortured' (v. 35) or 'faced jeers and flogging' (v. 36). Faith is as much expressed by those who cling to God in the middle of terrible hardships and limitations, as it is by those who take on risky ventures. Christians who live with depression or major disabilities, who have suffered awful bereavement, or for whom each day is a battle – they are the saints who will light up heaven. They cling to Christ when they have every reason to give up, and God will honour them for it.

- **Gives hope for the future.** For Old Testament saints the wait is a long time (vv. 39–40). They died in faith, without receiving their inheritance, waiting until the Gospel would come to us, so that only together with us would they partake in the new world God will bring about. So much of faith is a waiting game, but one day faith will turn to sight, our longings will be fulfilled, and we will reign with Christ in the New Jerusalem!

REFLECTION

How does faith transform a Christian's view of suffering?

READ Hebrews 12:1–11

In the movie *Dead Poets Society*, Robin Williams, playing the role of an unorthodox English teacher, takes his boys out of class and leads them down a corridor to an old grainy photograph of former pupils. These former pupils had lived their lives, and run their race. Now it was the turn of this new generation, and as the boys stare at the photograph, Robin Williams whispers to his class, '*Carpe diem*. Seize the day!'

Hebrews 11 is like an old grainy photograph of Old Testament saints who showed faith in God and overcame obstacles in their journey to the heavenly city. Now it's our turn! These Old Testament saints, cheering us on from the stands, teach us poignant lessons:

- **Run your race with perseverance.** The Christian life is like a race (v. 1), but not a sprint. It's more like a steeplechase with lots of obstacles, bumps and bruises along the way. Our biggest obstacle is our own sinful nature – not necessarily the grandiose sins of murder and adultery, but more subtle sins that are 'the sin that so easily entangles' us. Love of money, pleasure-seeking, and career aspirations all blunt our love for Christ. If we are to run with perseverance, we must get rid of the idols in our hearts, and fix our eyes on Christ, who endured a cross because of the glory that lay ahead of it (vv. 2–3).

- **Don't despise the discipline that's part of the race.** You cannot pursue Christ without suffering. But God uses suffering, in all its shapes and sizes, to 'discipline' us (v. 7). It is an indulgent father who refuses to discipline, but a loving father 'disciplines those he loves' (v. 6). William Carey saw years of Bible translation work in India going up in smoke when all his manuscripts were destroyed in a warehouse fire. But he saw God's hand in it, and acknowledged that arrogance had started to seep into his ministry. He exclaimed, 'The Lord has laid me low that I might look more simply to him.'

- **Discipline leads to holiness.** God's purpose in discipline is not to embitter us, but to refine us. Discipline is actually a sign of God's loving fatherhood, and if we submit to it, it 'produces a harvest of righteousness' (v. 11) in our lives. You can't be holy without discipline. Some Christians have become bitter, because they don't expect God to allow sometimes intense suffering. But when we see why God allows it, we will be better prepared to allow God's scalpel to shape our brokenness into the image of Christ.

REFLECTION

What has God's discipline produced in your life?

This passage is the culmination of a series of 'warning passages' in Hebrews. There are five warning passages, beginning back in chapter 2 with the danger of drifting, and now culminating in chapter 12 with Esau's complete denial of his glorious inheritance. Backsliding does not happen overnight. It begins with subtle compromise, taking your foot off the gas, but ends with completely forsaking the call of salvation.

This is poignantly pictured in the story of Esau 'who for a single meal sold his inheritance rights as the oldest son' (v. 16). The firstborn son in Israel held a privileged position. He was to be given a double share of the family inheritance. Esau should have known how precious his inheritance was, but when he returns home famished from a hunting trip and his devious brother Jacob has prepared a tantalising stew, Esau gives up his glorious inheritance for his favourite dish.

Esau's physical appetites got the better of him, and he gave up long-term blessing for short-term pleasure. And he is the tragic forefather of myriads of men and women, brought up in the church, who have tasted the goodness of the Gospel, and know that Christ died for sin, but have abandoned their rich heritage to pursue their own pleasures.

If Christ is as glorious as chapters 1–10 of Hebrews paint him to be; if he is the Son of God, creator of the universe, who became man to sympathise with us and to die so that his blood could save us from hell and catapult us to glory; if he is the judge of all the earth at the end times – then it is a desperately serious thing to turn your back on him to pursue your own pleasures.

Those pleasures aren't necessarily deeply evil things, any more than a tasty bowl of stew is a wicked thing in itself. The wickedness is in giving up the treasure that is Christ, to pursue other passions – whether it is making money, finding the girl or man of your dreams, or living a partying lifestyle. Sins such as these are the 'sin that ... entangles' (12:1), and can lead to forfeiting your heavenly inheritance.

Can you lose your salvation? Many other Bible passages would suggest not. True believers were chosen in Christ before the world began (Eph. 1:3–5). But if we are making no progress in our faith, and if we are cherishing other gods instead of Christ, then Hebrews wants to leave us feeling deeply uncomfortable, until we get on our knees and return to Christ. It is possible that such a person 'fails to obtain the grace of God' (v. 15, ESV).

REFLECTION

Are there idols in your life that are competing with Christ for allegiance?

The contrast between the old and new covenants is symbolised in this passage by two mountains – Mount Sinai, the literal, physical mountain where God gave the law to Israel, and Mount Zion, the spiritual, eternal mountain representing the kingdom of God.

Mount Sinai was a mountain shrouded in fear, as God appeared in 'fire ... darkness, gloom and storm' (v. 18, cf. Ex. 19:16–19) to bring the Ten Commandments to his old covenant people, Israel. Sinai was a fearful place because the God who appeared on the mountain was unapproachable due to human sin. If you even touched the foot of the mountain on which he appeared, you had to be stoned to death (v. 20, cf. Ex. 19:12–13).

That same God meets new covenant believers on the spiritual Mount Zion, but the meeting is much more joyous and liberating! Christ's blood has ensured that every Christian can now enter God's holy presence with confidence and boldness. Sin is dealt with, and every week when we worship on earth alongside God's people, we join this heavenly gathering of 'righteous men made perfect' (v. 23) and 'angels in joyful assembly' (v. 22) to worship God through the power of Jesus' sacrifice.

It's a scene that reminds me of Charles Wesley's great hymn 'And can it be that I should gain' with its words: 'Bold I approach the eternal throne, and claim the crown through Christ my own.'[6] God is no longer fenced off and fearful. He is Father, and he invites us to come and worship in the heavenly sanctuary that used to have barbed wire placed around it.

But the joy of the heavenly Zion does not mean we can treat our place in this new kingdom lightly (vv. 25–29). We cannot approach our Saviour in any old way, but 'with reverence and awe' (v. 28), acknowledging the price that was paid to get us here – the blood of Christ – and the fact that God is as holy as he has always been.

Our salvation has not been purchased because God has lowered his standards – deciding to be softer on sin in the New Testament age than he was in the Old. Not at all! God has dealt with sin ferociously, but his fury has been poured out on Christ, and grace is ours. It's not cheap grace brought on by a relaxation of holiness, but costly grace achieved through the death of the Son of God, 'for our "God is [still] a consuming fire"' (v. 29).

REFLECTION

Do you worship God as if he were a 'consuming fire'?

 [6] Wesley, Charles (1707-78), *And can it be that I should gain*

Hebrews is a book that begins like a sermon, and ends like a letter. Often you will find at the end of New Testament letters a list of practical exhortations that are not linked with the main argument of the letter, but apply to every Christian, for all time. And the exhortations Hebrews chooses are very relevant:

• **Love your brothers.** We do that not just sentimentally with hugs and kisses, but practically by showing hospitality to those who need it, and by standing alongside those who are suffering – in the Hebrews' case, those who were in prison. Love is not about words or emotions, but practical service to one another.

• **Honour marriage.** With divorce statistics within the church as rife as in the secular world, we need to keep faithful to our spouse. 'God will judge the adulterer and all the sexually immoral' (v. 4), and Christians are no more immune to sexual unfaithfulness than King David, the writer of Psalms, who observed Bathsheba from his balcony in the pale moonlight (2 Sam. 11). We betray our marriages, not just through affairs, but through computer screens! Keep our heart pure.

• **Be content.** Having money isn't a problem, but loving it is! We are to 'be content with what you have' (v. 5), knowing that God is enough, wealth is fleeting, and heaven is more glorious than we can imagine. Don't store up treasure here – if you're wealthy, give unusual amounts to God's kingdom and watch it transform the hopes of the poor. Store up treasure in heaven where your stocks and shares are always on the rise!

• **Respect your leaders.** The command of verses 7–8 isn't asking us to obey leaders whatever they do, for leaders fail as much as anyone. But it is effectively saying, 'Put into practice whatever good you see in your leaders, and pray for them as men who must give account.' Make your leader's job a pleasure, not a headache!

Of course the ultimate question is 'Why should we keep all these moral commands?' This isn't about doing good to earn God's favour. We already have God's favour in Christ. No, we do all these good works because 'Jesus Christ is the same yesterday and today and for ever' (v. 8). Our good works are a response to his grace, his greatness, his love and his beauty. Good works are not our way to heaven; they are our thanks for the one who got us there! We are saved by grace, but we also live by grace every day.

REFLECTION

Do you love in word only, or also in deeds?

In this closing passage, the writer invites his readers to contrast the present 'Jerusalem' they are living in, with the future 'Jerusalem' they are actually part of. Life in this world will always be full of false religion and alienation for Christians who are truly following Christ, but our rejection of false religion and our alienation from the culture are signs that we truly are children of the New Jerusalem.

The passage begins by talking, quite obliquely, about false teaching, which has something to do with ceremonial food laws. The coming of Christ has meant that following food laws and particular religious rituals to make you right with God has been replaced by God's grace in Christ: 'It is good for our hearts to be strengthened by grace, not by ceremonial foods' (v. 9). False religion will always tell us to fulfil certain rituals as the way to be right with God. But we are children of grace, accepted by God already on the basis of Christ's sacrifice, and we need to shun any teaching that drags us back into a world of empty ritual. That's part of the Old Jerusalem, but we now have New Jerusalem passports.

Of course when we dance to the tunes of grace rather than ritual, we will not be welcome, and the writer reminds his readers how Christ himself was crucified 'outside the camp' (v. 11).

Outside the city walls of Jerusalem, rejected by the Judaism of his day, Christ died in shame. But the writer says we must go to him 'outside the camp', and be willing to face the shame and reproach he experienced. We don't belong to this world anymore: 'we do not have an enduring city, but we are looking for the city that is to come' (v. 14).

Our eyes are not fixed on the short-term joys of this world. We are now active citizens of the world to come: Mount Zion packed with a multitude of angels in joyful assembly. That's where we belong! So we live life today according to the values of Zion: 'let us continually offer to God a sacrifice' – not of bulls and goats, but 'of praise … And do not forget to do good and to share with others' (vv. 15-16). The sacrifices God really appreciates, now that Christ's blood has been shed 'once for all', are lips that praise God and lives that pursue good works, loving our brothers and sisters. We are children of the future, living as a signpost of the age to come.

REFLECTION

Are you living for this world or the next? How do you know?

Being a leader is hard going. I've been a pastor and an elder for fourteen years, and I am sure I have made many mistakes in my time, but more often than not I have tried my best to serve God and serve his people! Being led is also not easy, when we have our own views on how church should be, and sometimes find leaders deciding things that we do not feel are good but we have little power to change.

But this passage teaches us that we need to respect our leaders: 'Obey your leaders and submit to their authority' (v. 17). Sometimes they will get things wrong, but they are more likely to be the people God wants them to be if they have our support and encouragement. Whatever we think of our leaders, in the cold light of day we would admit that every church needs people appointed and gifted to lead the church, and that is a hard job! The job of the leader is not to lord it over his people, or manipulate them to get what he wants, but to lead with a servant heart (1 Pet. 5:1–4).

The job of church members is to submit to that leadership to make our leaders' life a joy and not a tribulation: 'Let them do this with joy and not with groaning' (v. 17, ESV). Notice that the job of leaders is not to please us, but to guard our soul: 'for they are keeping watch over your souls' (v. 17, ESV). This involves spurring us on, and driving the church on to be more effective witnesses to the Gospel. If we have leaders who are doing that, let's celebrate them and thank them, no matter how uncomfortable it sometimes makes life for us! Since when was discipleship ever comfortable?

But the church is not just about leaders teaching and envisioning. Leaders are here to 'prepare God's people for works of service' (Eph. 4:12). There isn't just one minister in a church – every member is a minister, or, as Peter puts it, we are 'a chosen race, a royal priesthood, a holy nation' (1 Pet. 2:9, ESV). That's why every member of Christ's church needs empowering, not to sit in a pew, but to live the Gospel out in the world: 'May the God of peace ... equip you with everything good for doing his will, and may he work in us what is pleasing to him, through Jesus Christ, to whom be glory for ever and ever. Amen' (vv. 20–21).

REFLECTION

How can you show gratitude to your leaders in church?

31

It would be a bit of an anticlimax to end our thoughts on this wonderful letter to the Hebrews on the rather abrupt thought of 'obey your leaders'. So let's go back to the beginning and these wonderful verses about the supremacy of Christ, and remind ourselves what this letter has been all about.

Jesus is the culmination of God's plan to save us. All the prophets of the Old Testament were preparing the way for God's Son to come into the world to achieve what no Old Testament hero or institution could achieve in itself. God has become fully human in Jesus, so that he could die for our sin on the cross, and live such an authentic human life that he can sympathise with us, and help us cope with the temptations and suffering we face today.

The Son of God, who upholds the entire universe by his powerful word, has now got so close to us by becoming fully human that he can be our great High Priest, greater than any Old Testament priest. As a priest he has offered a 'once for all' sacrifice by shedding his blood on the cross, a sacrifice that is better than all the Old Testament ones because it cleanses us from all sin in a real way, not a symbolic way, and because since it is the blood of God, it can deal with our sin forever, not temporarily like Old Testament animal sacrifices.

So as forgiven sons and daughters of God, we come into God's presence not like those who trembled at Mount Sinai but with joy, knowing that our sins are covered, that Jesus understands our weaknesses and prays for us before God's throne, and that we receive a welcome from a holy God who has now become our Father through Jesus. We pray to him and live for him as children of grace.

And we are now called to 'fix our eyes' (12:2) on Jesus, being content to follow his example and to live for his glory even though we cannot see him. Our obedience to God will involve suffering, as it did for Jesus. But just as his suffering gave way to glory, so will ours. So let's keep following him with all our hearts, knowing that there is an eternal city built by God, a city of joy, which is waiting for all those who follow Jesus and are prepared to shun the attractions of this life to take their place in the heavenly Jerusalem that is coming!

REFLECTION

How is your life and your thinking going to change as a result of studying Hebrews?